BEAUTIFUL BEASTS

PLATYHYSTRIX

POTAMOTHERIUM

SORDES

Written by Camilla de la Bedoyere
Managing Editor: Laura Knowles
Designer: Clare Barker
Art Director: Susi Martin
Publisher: Zeta Jones
Associate Publisher: Maxime Boucknooghe
Production: Nikki Ingram

First published in the UK in 2014 by Marshall Editions

A catalogue record for this book is available from the British Library.

ISBN 978-1-78493-028-8

Originated in Hong Kong by Cypress Colours (HK) Ltd
Printed and bound in China
by 1010 Printing International Ltd

10 9 8 7 6 5 4 3 2 1   14 15 16 17 18

DUNCLEOSTEOUS

HOMALODOTHERIUM

LESOTHOSARUS

HEART-NOSED BAT

PISTOSAURUS

BEAUTIFUL BEASTS

A Collection of Creatures
PAST AND PRESENT

DSUNGARIPTERUS

THYLACOLEO

BRONTOTHERIUM

PLATYPUS

In a time gone by..

From mighty mammoths to terrifying pteranodons, the story of life on Earth is one of beautiful beasts in an ever-changing world.

Once upon a time, the world was a very different place. The animals that lived on prehistoric Earth didn't look like the ones we see in our forests, fields and oceans today. There were massive slithering snakes, hairy rhinos, bone-crunching armoured fish and ferocious dinosaurs that ruled the land. In this book, we have collected together a range of extraordinary and beautiful beasts that lived in many different times and places.

FROM TIME TO TIME

The Earth has existed for about 4.6 billion years. At first, it was a burning, exploding, landless and lifeless place. The story of life began in the oceans, about 3.5 billion years ago. This amazing story is divided into chapters of geological time called eras, periods and epochs. Dividing up time into big chunks makes it easier to understand the way the world has changed, and work out when animals and plants lived and died. Each chunk of time is given a name, such as "Jurassic" or "Eocene" and can be put on a timeline, in order from the past to present.

TIMELINE

mya = 'millions of years ago'

405 mya — the first wingless insects
380 mya — the first tree-like plants
230 mya — the first dinosaurs
210 mya — the first mammals

ERA	PALEOZOIC						MESOZ
PERIOD/EPOCH	CAMBRIAN	ORDOVICIAN	SILURIAN	DEVONIAN	CARBONIFEROUS	PERMIAN	TRIASSIC	JURASSIC

540 mya · 485 mya · 445 mya · 420 mya · 360 mya · 300 mya · 250 mya · 205 mya

470 mya — the first land plants

510 mya — the first fish

335 mya — the first amphibians

310 mya — the first reptiles

150 mya — the first birds

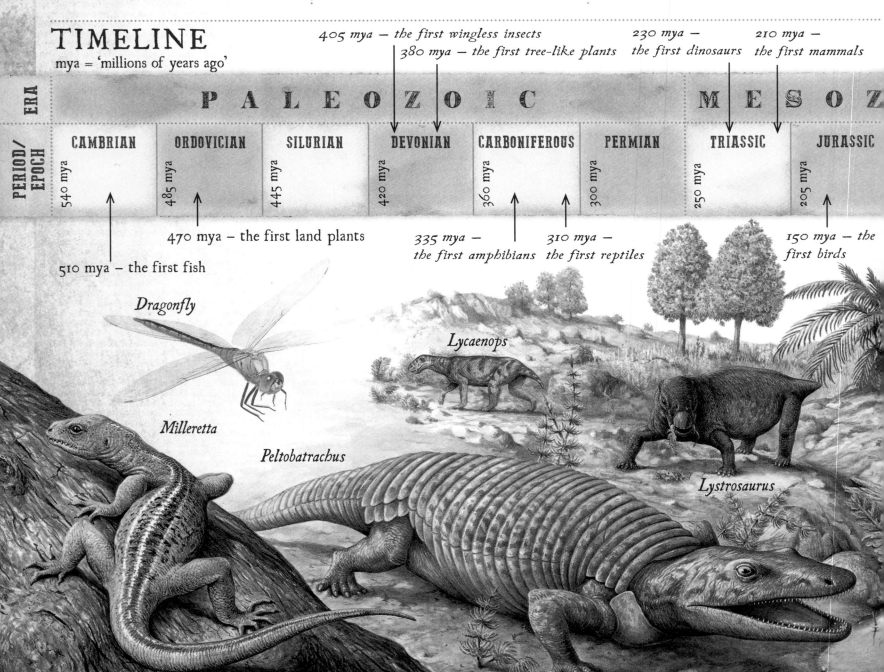

Dragonfly

Milleretta

Peltobatrachus

Lycaenops

Lystrosaurus

ALL THINGS CHANGE

Over millions of years, the world's climate has kept changing, as have the positions of the continents (large areas of land). During some periods, such as the Cambrian and the Triassic periods, the world was much hotter than it is today. During the Devonian – a time known as the Age of Fishes – the sea levels were very high and all the land was clustered around the South Pole. More recently, in the Eocene, an enormous ice sheet began to spread over the Antarctic.

By 10 million years ago, the whole world began to cool and eventually many lands and seas became covered in thick layers of ice and snow.

EXTINCTION

As the world has changed so have animals and plants. They have to change to survive, and that change is called evolution. Those that do not successfully adapt to a new climate or other changing conditions die out. When a type of animal, or plant, dies out forever it has gone extinct. Evolution and extinction are normal events in the world's history and have led to the huge variety of incredible living things on Earth.

There have been at least five times in the Earth's history when many animals and plants have died out in a very short time. These are called mass extinction events (MEEs). The most famous of all MEEs was the K-T Extinction at the end of the Cretaceous period. The dinosaurs went extinct, but their disappearance meant that mammals could thrive in their place.

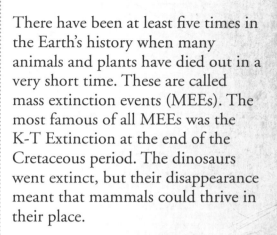

200,000 years ago —
the first humans: Homo sapiens

Present day

| D I C | C E N O Z O I C | | | | | | | | |

CRETACEOUS	PALAEOCENE	EOCENE	OLIGOCENE	MIOCENE	PLIOCENE	PLEISTOCENE	RECENT
145 mya	65 mya	55 mya	34 mya	24 mya	5 mya	2.5 mya	12,000 years ago

65 mya – mass extinction event

125 mya – the first flowering plants

Robertia

Dicynodon

Procynosuchus

Lycaenops

Animals with Armour

Built like tanks, these armour-plated beasts can afford to be fearless. Who's tough enough to take a bite?

PANOPLOSAURUS
Late Cretaceous
Pan-OP-lo-SAW-rus

DESMATOSUCHUS
Late Triassic
dez-MAT-oh-SOO-kus

STEGOSAURUS
Late Jurassic
STEG-oh-SAW-rus

COLOSSOCHELYS
Miocene to Pliocene
koh-LOSS-oh-kel-is

PINK FAIRY ARMADILLO
Modern

DOEDICURUS
Pleistocene
day-dik-YOO-rus

HENODUS
Late Triassic
HEN-oh-dus

HYLAEOSAURUS
Early Cretaceous
hy-LEE-oh-SAW-rus

GROENLANDASPIS
Devonian
grohn-LAN-das-PIS

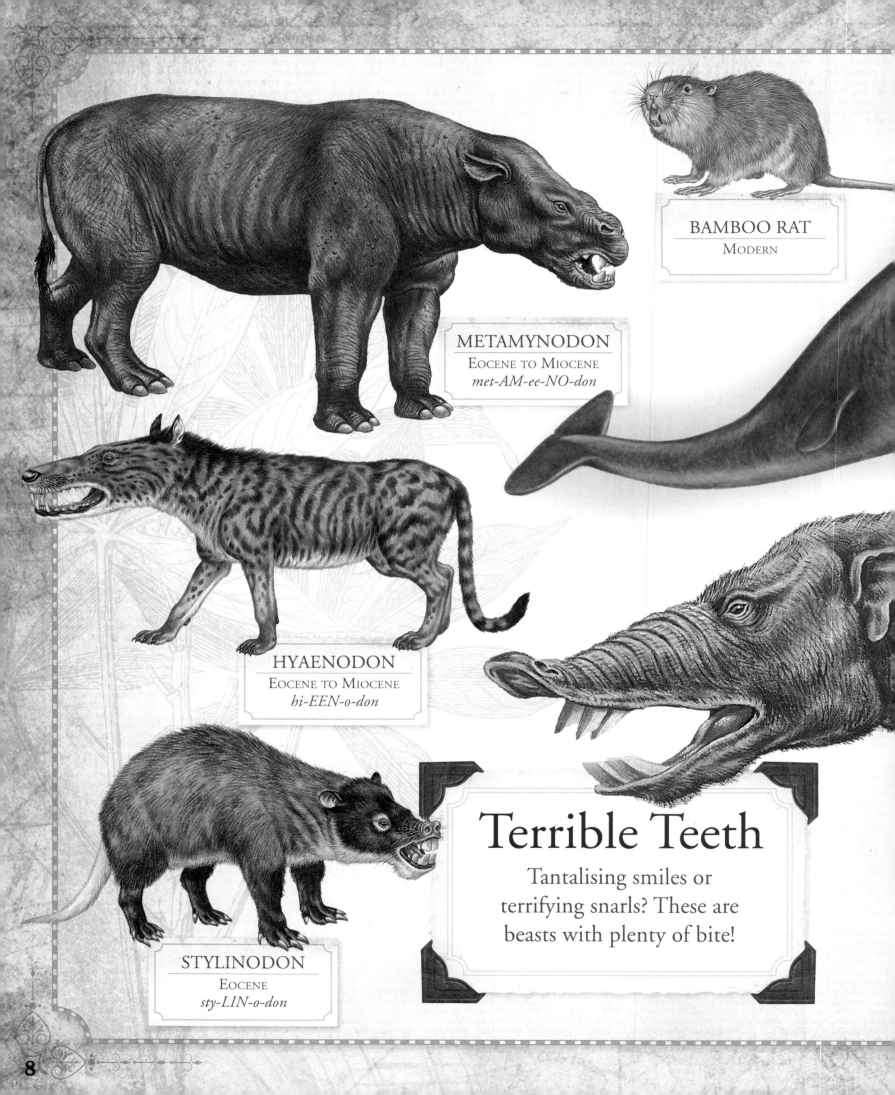

BAMBOO RAT
MODERN

METAMYNODON
EOCENE TO MIOCENE
met-AM-ee-NO-don

HYAENODON
EOCENE TO MIOCENE
hi-EEN-o-don

STYLINODON
EOCENE
sty-LIN-o-don

Terrible Teeth

Tantalising smiles or terrifying snarls? These are beasts with plenty of bite!

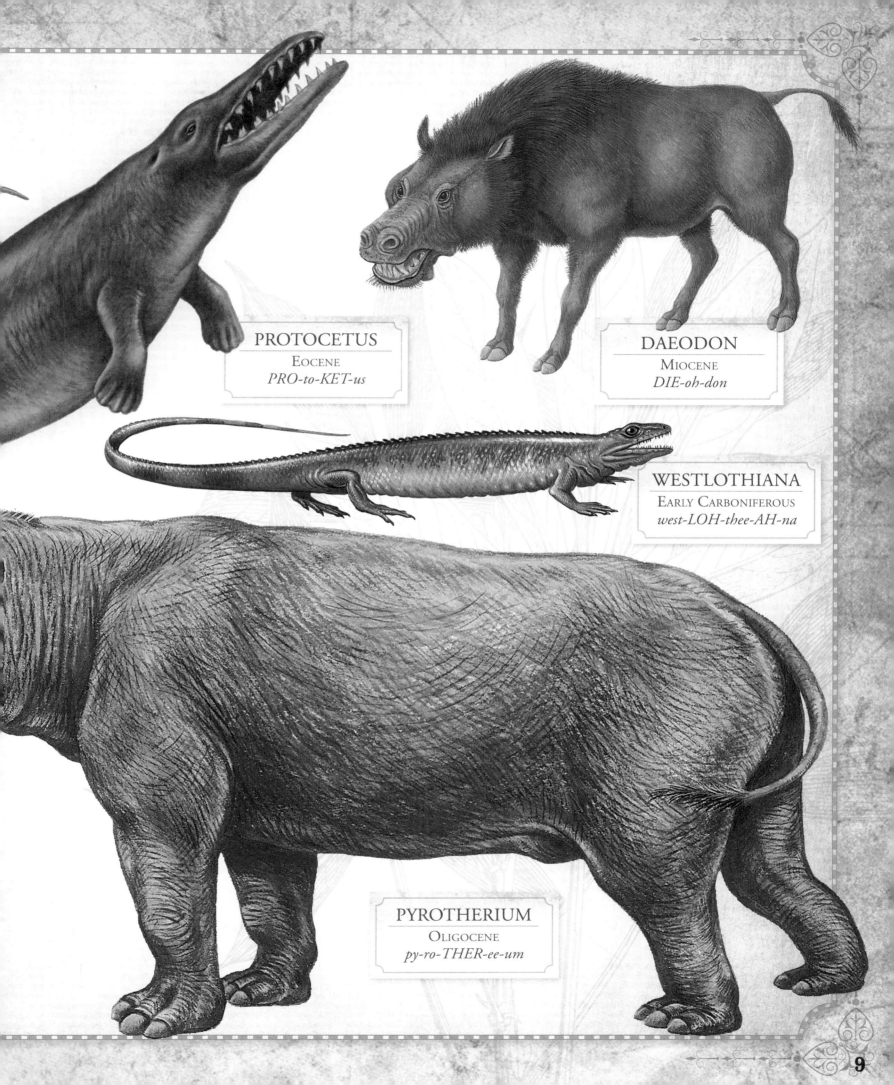

PROTOCETUS
Eocene
PRO-to-KET-us

DAEODON
Miocene
DIE-oh-don

WESTLOTHIANA
Early Carboniferous
west-LOH-thee-AH-na

PYROTHERIUM
Oligocene
py-ro-THER-ee-um

On the Hoof

These fleet-footed animals are related to modern horses, cattle, deer and camels.

HYRACOTHERIUM
Eocene
hy-rack-o-THER-ee-um

PALAEOTHERIUM
Eocene
pay-lee-oh-THER-ee-um

PRZEWALSKI'S HORSE
Modern

CAMELOPS
Pliocene to Pleistocene
CAM-ell-lops

HIPPIDION
Pleistocene
hip-i-DEE-on

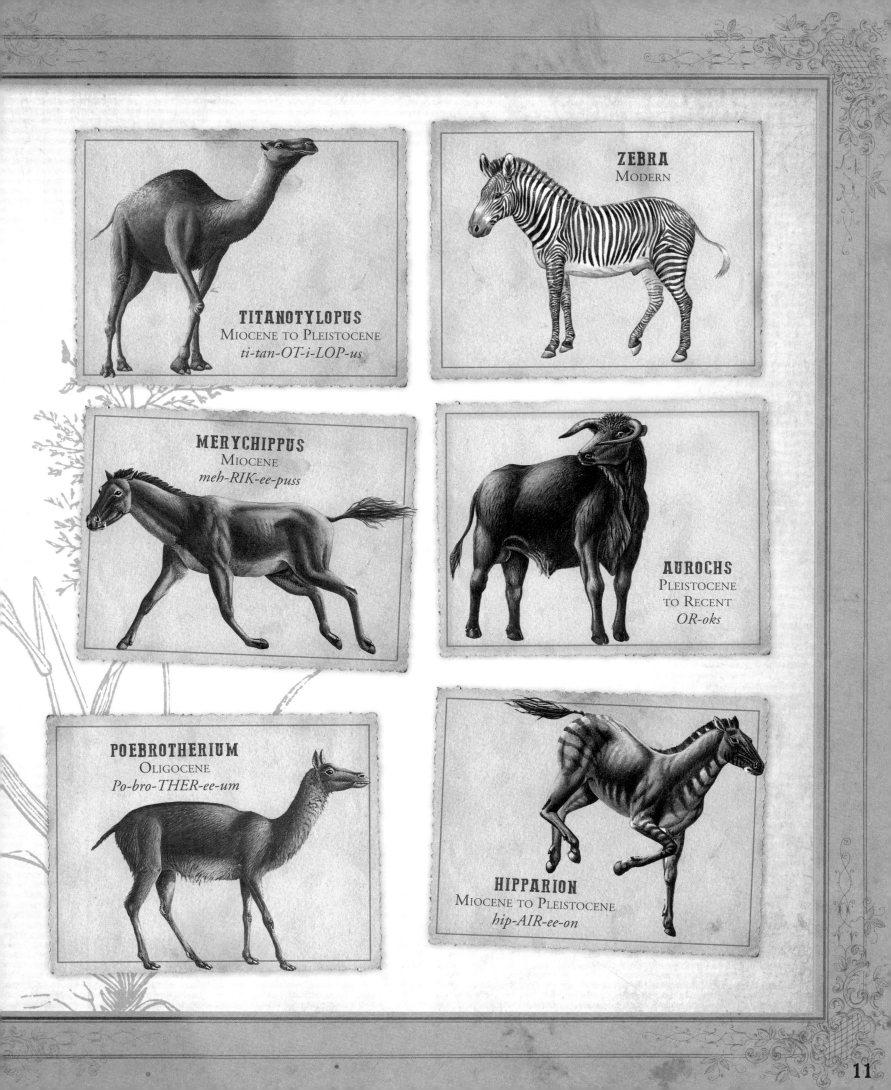

TITANOTYLOPUS
Miocene to Pleistocene
ti-tan-OT-i-LOP-us

ZEBRA
Modern

MERYCHIPPUS
Miocene
meh-RIK-ee-puss

AUROCHS
Pleistocene
to Recent
OR-oks

POEBROTHERIUM
Oligocene
Po-bro-THER-ee-um

HIPPARION
Miocene to Pleistocene
hip-AIR-ee-on

SIAMOTYRANNUS
EARLY CRETACEOUS
sigh-AM-oh-tie-ran-us

KOMODO
DRAGON
MODERN

ALBERTOSAURUS
LATE CRETACEOUS
al-bert-oh-SAW-rus

Which of these
ferocious reptiles has
a venomous bite?

Terrible Tyrants

Many different reptiles have walked the Earth, but dinosaurs were the biggest and scariest. The name 'dinosaur' means terrible lizard.

CALLOVOSAURUS
Middle Jurassic
cal-OH-vo-SAW-rus

ALIORAMUS
Late Cretaceous
al-ee-or-A-mus

TYRANNOSAURUS
Late Cretaceous
ti-RAN-oh-SAW-rus

Speedy Swimmers

Speed is one super survival trick, and swimmers make the most of it.

ASPIDORHYNCHUS
Late Jurassic
as-PI-dor-RIN-cus

PALAEONISCUM
Permian
PAY-lee-oh-NIS-cum

PERLEIDUS
Triassic
PER-lay-DUS

SAURICHTHYS
Triassic
saw-RIK-this

GREERERPETON
Carboniferous
GREE-rer-PEH-ton

GOLDFISH
Modern

ENCHODUS
Cretaceous to Eocene
en-KOH-dus

PLATECARPUS
Late Cretaceous
PLAT-ee-CAR-pus

HYPSIDORIS
Eocene
HIP-si-DOR-is

Huge Horns

Used for attack, defence or courtship, these horns make an amazing display.

EOBASILEUS
Eocene
eo-bas-il-AY-us

ELGINIA
Permian
eli-GIN-ee-ah

MONTANOCERATOPS
Late Cretaceous
mon-TAN-oh-ser-a-tops

ELASMOTHERIUM
Pliocene to Pleistocene
el-AS-mo-THER-ee-um

JACKSON'S
CHAMELEON

Modern

AMERICAN
BUFFALO

Modern

STYRACOSAURUS

Late Cretaceous
sty-rak-oh-SAW-rus

EMBOLOTHERIUM

Eocene
EM-bol-o-THER-ee-um

OSTEODONTORNIS

MIOCENE
OST-ee-oh-don-TORN-is

ARCHAEOPTERYX

LATE JURASSIC TO
EARLY CRETACEOUS
ark-ee-OP-ter-iks

Peculiar Birds

Strange beaks and fabulous
feathers were not enough
to protect most of these birds
from extinction.

HELMETED
HORNBILL

MODERN

DIATRYMA

EOCENE
Die-ah-tree-ma

DODO

MODERN (EXTINCT)

LAMINATED
TOUCAN
MODERN

GREAT AUK
MODERN (EXTINCT)

Two of these
birds had teeth!
Can you spot
which ones?

GIANT MOA
MODERN (EXTINCT)

ARGENTAVIS
MIOCENE
ar-jen-TAY-vis

19

PACHYCEPHALOSAURUS
Late Cretaceous
PAK-ee-KEF-a-loh-SAW-rus

ACANTHOSTEGA
Devonian
ah-CAN-thoh-STAY-ga

ANATOSAURUS
Late Cretaceous
an-at-oh-SAW-rus

Funny Faces

Beauty is in the eye of the beholder. Some beasts have a face only a mother could love.

DILOPHOSAURUS
Early Jurassic
die-LOAF-oh-SAW-rus

PROBOSCIS MONKEY
Modern

CRASSIGYRINUS
Carboniferous
KRA-sig-i-RIN-us

GERROTHORAX
Late Triassic
GEH-roh-THOR-ax

TSINTAOSAURUS
Late Cretaceous
CHING-dow-SAW-rus

MIACIS
Palaeocene to Eocene
my-AH-sis

CRUSAFONTIA
Early Cretaceous
croos-a-FONT-ee-a

MEGAZOSTRODON
Late Triassic to Early Jurassic
meg-a-ZOST-roh-don

EUROPEAN RABBIT
Modern

NECROLESTES
Miocene
nec-ro-LES-tes

Mini Mammals

The first mammals lived about 200 million years ago. They were small and furry.

HARAMIYA
Late Triassic to Early Jurassic
har-a-MEE-ya

ZALAMBDALESTES
Late Cretaceous
zal-am-dal-EST-es

PTILODUS
Palaeocene
til-oh-dus

ALPHADON
Late Cretaceous to Eocene
ALF-a-don

PURGATORIUS
Palaeocene
purg-a-TOR-ee-us

METACHEIROMYS
Eocene
meta-KIR-oh-mis

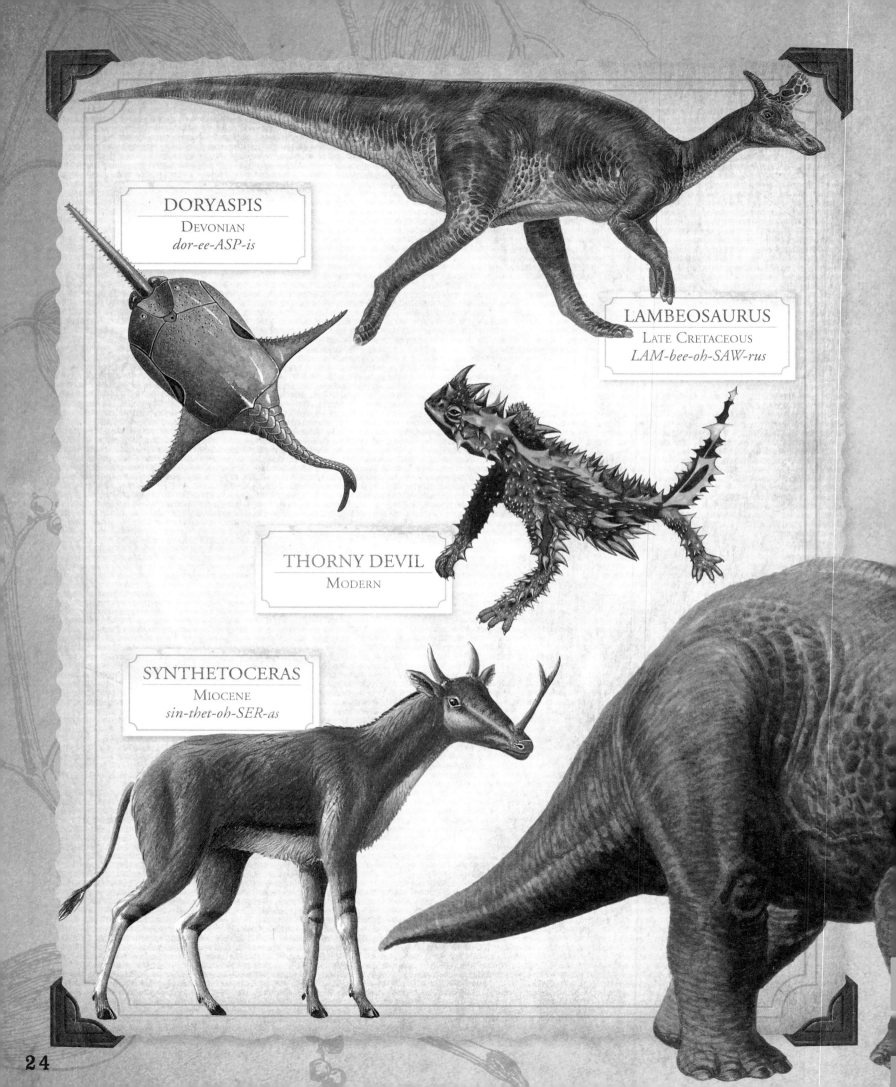

DORYASPIS
Devonian
dor-ee-ASP-is

LAMBEOSAURUS
Late Cretaceous
LAM-bee-oh-SAW-rus

THORNY DEVIL
Modern

SYNTHETOCERAS
Miocene
sin-thet-oh-SER-as

SPINY TAILED SKINK
MODERN

SCLERORHYNCHUS
LATE CRETACEOUS
skleh-roh-RIN-kuss

ELGINIA
PERMIAN
el-GIN-ee-ah

Strange Spikes
These bony bits, hard horns and super-large scales and spikes are not just for decoration.

STYRACOSAURUS
EARLY CRETACEOUS
sty-RAK-oh-SAW-rus

PROGANOCHELYS
LATE TRIASSIC
pro-gan-oh-KEEL-is

25

Masters of the Air

See these aerial acrobats swoop, soar, glide, flit and flap through the skies.

ANUROGNATHUS

Late Jurassic

ann-yew-ro-KNAY-thus

ICARONYCTERIS

Eocene

Ik-a-roh-NIK-ter-is

DIMORPHODON

Early Jurassic

dy-MORF-oh-don

GREAT BLACK-BACKED GULL

Modern

QUETZALCOATLUS
LATE CRETACEOUS
kwet-zal-coh-at-lus

PTERANODON
LATE CRETACEOUS
teh-RAN-oh-don

KUEHNEOSAURUS
LATE TRIASSIC
kew-nee-oh-SAW-rus

RHAMPHORHYNCHUS
LATE JURASSIC
RAM-for-INK-us

Which of these fluffy fliers was an ancient type of bat?

DSUNGARIPTERUS
EARLY CRETACEOUS
SUNG-a-RIPT-er-us

SCAPHOGNATHUS
LATE JURASSIC
skaf-oh-KNAY-thus

DIMETRODON
Permian
di-MEE-troh-don

Bizarre Bodies
Animals, from prehistory to today, come in many shapes and sizes. It takes all sorts!

LONGISQUAMA
Middle to Late Triassic
LON-gee-skwa-ma

CORYTHOSAURUS
Late Cretaceous
ko-RITH-oh-SAW-rus

Which of these creatures used its strange shape to keep warm?

DIPLOCAULUS
PERMIAN
dip-lo-KAW-lus

OURANOSAURUS
CRETACEOUS
OO-ran-oh-SAW-rus

EOMANIS
EOCENE
eo-MAN-is

FRILLED LIZARD
MODERN

PARASAUROLOPHUS
LATE CRETACEOUS
PARA-saw-ROL-oh-fus

JAGUAR

Modern

COELURUS

Late Jurassic to Early Cretaceous

see-loo-rus

PLANOCEPHALOSAURUS

Late Triassic

PLAN-oh-KEF-al-oh-SAW-rus

TERRESTRISUCHUS

Late Triassic

ter-EST-ri-SOOK-us

HAPALOPS

Miocene

HAP-al-ops

Spots and Speckles

These beauties are gorgeous in their coats, scales and skins of many colours.

BOROPHAGUS

MIOCENE TO PLIOCENE

bo-ro-fay-gus

PLANETETHERIUM

PALAEOCENE

PLAN-et-ee-THER-ee-um

GEMUENDINA

DEVONIAN

JEM-oo-en-DEE-na

NORTHERN LEOPARD FROG

MODERN

COELUROSAURAVUS
Permian
see-lur-OH-saw-AY-vus

HYPSILOPHODON
Early Cretaceous
hy-RAK-oh-don

VELOCIRAPTOR
Late Cretaceous
vel-O-si-RAP-tor

LIOPLEURODON
Middle to Late Jurassic
LIE-oh-PLER-oh-don

Can you spot which of these creatures travelled by gliding?

MOSASAURUS
Late Cretaceous
moh-za-SAW-rus

THOATHERIUM
Miocene
tho-ath-ER-ee-um

LEPTICTIDIUM
Eocene
LEP-tic-TID-ee-um

RUBY-THROATED
HUMMINGBIRD
MODERN

OSTRICH
MODERN

Fast Movers

Beasts need to get from
A to B to find food, water,
shelter and mates.

HYRACODON
EOCENE TO OLIGOCENE
hi-RAK-oh-don

33

ECHINODON
EARLY CRETACEOUS
eh-KY-no-don

ORNITHOSUCHUS
LATE TRIASSIC
OR-nith-oh-SOOK-us

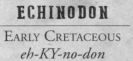

GREAT JERBOA
MODERN

Two Feet

Because of the shape of their hip bones, some beasts walk on four legs while others use just two.

PRENOCEPHALE
LATE CRETACEOUS
pren-oh-KEF-a-lee

HETERODONTOSAURUS

Early Jurassic
HET-er-oh-DONT-oh-SAW-rus

MASSOSPONDYLUS

Late Triassic to Early Jurassic
MASS-oh-SPOND-i-lus

EUPARKERIA

Early Triassic
YOO-park-EE-ree-a

SINOSAUROPTERYX

Early Cretaceous
SIGH-no-saw-OP-ter-iks

PROCOPTODON

Pleistocene
pro-COP-toh-don

Mighty Mammoths

The most magnificent of all mammals, these are members of the elephant family.

DEINOTHERIUM
Miocene to Early Pleistocene
dine-o-THER-ee-um

ASTRAPOTHERIUM
Oligocene to Miocene
ast-rap-oh-THER-ee-um

MAMMUTHUS MERIDIONALIS
Pleistocene
ma-mu-thus mer-id-ee-on-AL-is

Which of these giants lived in the coldest places?

WOOLLY MAMMOTH
PLEISTOCENE TO RECENT

AMEBELODON
MIOCENE
am-eh-BEL-oh-don

Nibblers and Grazers

It takes strong jaws and tough teeth to munch through grass, seeds and nuts.

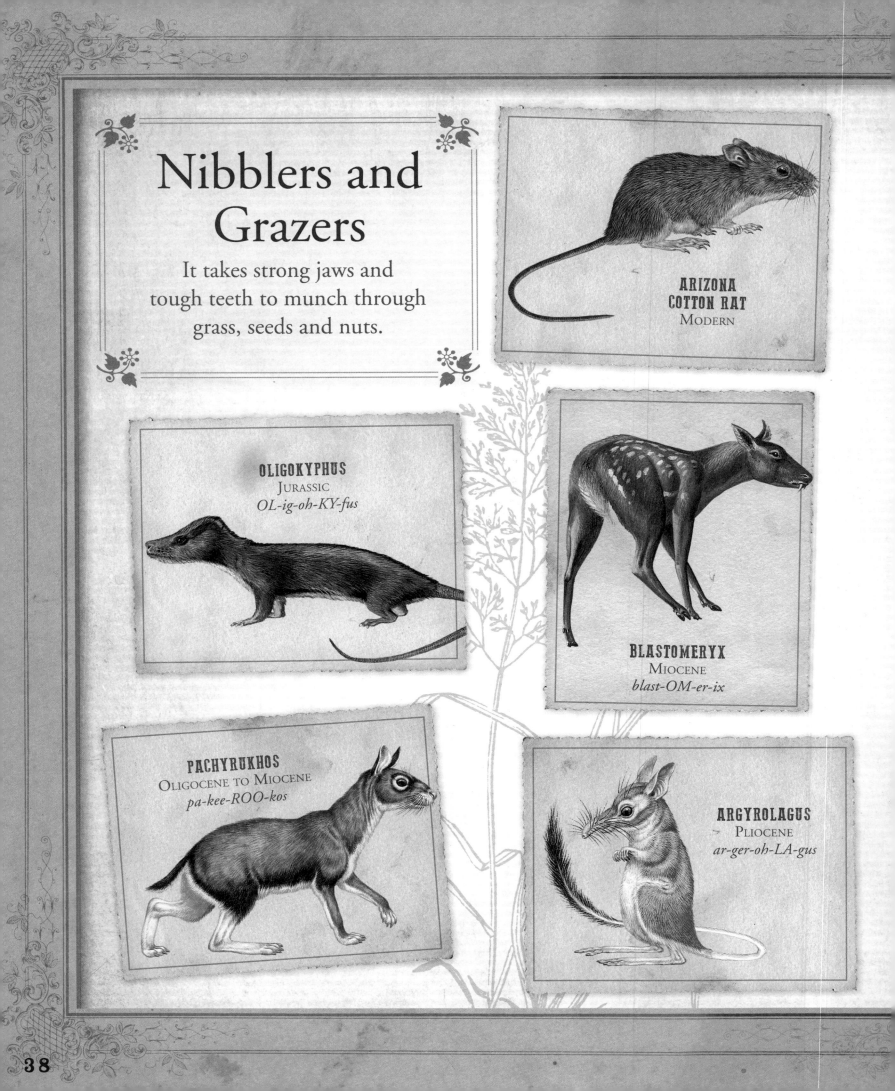

ARIZONA COTTON RAT
Modern

OLIGOKYPHUS
Jurassic
OL-ig-oh-KY-fus

BLASTOMERYX
Miocene
blast-OM-er-ix

PACHYRUKHOS
Oligocene to Miocene
pa-kee-ROO-kos

ARGYROLAGUS
Pliocene
ar-ger-oh-LA-gus

PROTYPOTHERIUM
Miocene
PRO-tip-o-THER-ee-um

AFRICAN ASS
Modern

RHYNCHIPPUS
Eocene to
Oligocene
rin-kip-us

EOCARDIA
Miocene
ee-oh-CARD-ee-a

CERATOGAULUS
Miocene to Pliocene
SER-at-oh-GOW-lus

PALAEOLAGUS
Eocene to Oligocene
pay-lee-oh-LA-gus

PLEUROSAURUS
Late Jurassic
PLOO-roh-SAW-rus

PROTARCHAEOPTERYX
Early Cretaceous
pro-TARK-ee-OP-ter-iks

EUOPLOCEPHALUS
Late Cretaceous
you-op-loh-KEF-ah-lus

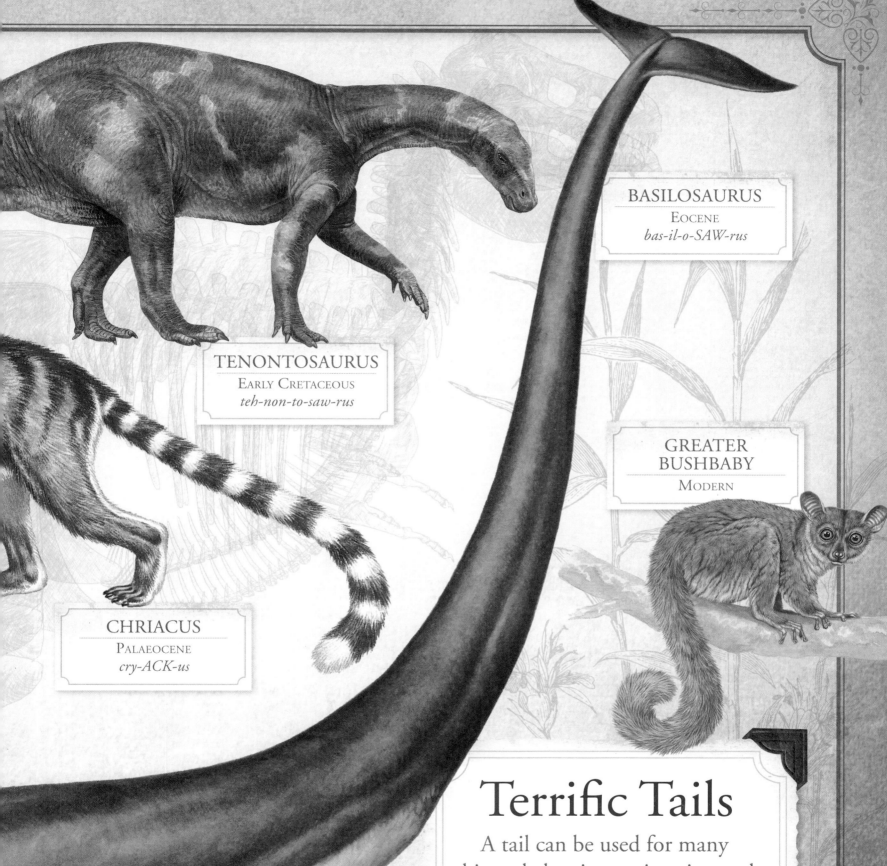

BASILOSAURUS
Eocene
bas-il-o-SAW-rus

TENONTOSAURUS
Early Cretaceous
teh-non-to-saw-rus

GREATER
BUSHBABY
Modern

CHRIACUS
Palaeocene
cry-ACK-us

Terrific Tails

A tail can be used for many things: balancing, swimming and even whacking other animals!

Incredible Hulks

When size is on your side
there is little to fear.
Big is beautiful!

HIPPOPOTAMUS

MODERN

BARAPASAURUS

EARLY JURASSIC
ba-RA-pa-SAW-rus

42

RIOJASAURUS

Late Triassic
ree-okah-SAW-rus

BRACHIOSAURUS

Late Jurassic
BRACK-ee-oh-SAW-rus

PLATEOSAURUS

Late Triassic
PLAT-ee-oh-SAW-rus

ARSINOITHERIUM

Early Oligocene
ars-in-oy-THER-ee-um

Slippery Skin

With slimy skin and smooth scales, these creatures are built for slipping and sliding through the weeds and reeds.

KERATERPETON
Carboniferous
ker-at-eh-PET-on

PANTYLUS
Early Permian
pan-TIE-lus

VIERAELLA
Early Jurassic
VI-er-RAY-la

PALAEOBATRACHUS
Cretaceous to Miocene
PAY-lee-oh-ba-TRA-kus

OPHIDERPETON
Carboniferous to Permian
oh-fi-DER-peh-ton

TRIADOBATRACHUS
Early Triassic
TRY-ad-oh-ba-TRA-kus

MICROBRACHIS
Carboniferous
MY-kro-BRAK-is

PHLEGETHONTIA
Carboniferous to Permian
FLE-geh-THON-tee-ah

KARAURUS
Late Jurassic
ka-RAW-rus

PACHYRHACHIS
Late Cretaceous
PAK-ee-RAK-iss

ARCHAEOTHERIUM
Eocene to Oligocene
ARK-ee-oh-THER-ee-um

COELOPHYSIS
Triassic to Jurassic
seel-oh-FY-sis

ORNITHOMIMUS
Late Cretaceous
ORN-ith-oh-MIM-us

Can you tell which of these beasts were hunters?

DIACODEXIS
Eocene
dee-a-co-DEX-is

COBELODUS

PERMIAN
COB-e-LOH-dus

Super Stripes

In the right environment,
stylish stripes can help
you hide.

CLADOSICTIS

LATE OLIGOCENE TO EARLY MIOCENE
CLAY-doh-sik-tis

INDIAN STRIPED
PALM SQUIRREL

MODERN

HYPACROSAURUS

LATE CRETACEOUS
hi-PAK-ro-saw-rus

PLESIOSAURUS
Late Jurassic
PLEEZ-ee-oh-SAW-rus

SMOOTH HAMMERHEAD
Modern

PIRANHA
Modern

MACROPLATA
Early Jurassic
mac-roh-PLAT-a

ELASMOSAURUS
LATE CRETACEOUS
el-az-mo-SAW-rus

MESOSAURUS
PERMIAN
MES-oh-SAW-rus

Danger Below

Underneath the rippling surface of the water, danger lurks in the form of these hungry hunters.

ICHTHYOSAURUS
LATE TRIASSIC TO EARLY CRETACEOUS
IK-thee-oh-SAW-rus

SHONISAURUS
LATE TRIASSIC
SHOH-nee-SAW-rus

PLESICTIS
OLIGOCENE TO MIOCENE
ples-IK-tis

CHAPALMALANIA
PLIOCENE
CHAP-al-mal-AN-ee-a

TOXODON
MIOCENE TO PLEISTOCENE
TOX-o-don

PHLAOCYON
OLIGOCENE TO MIOCENE
phlay-oh-SIGH-on

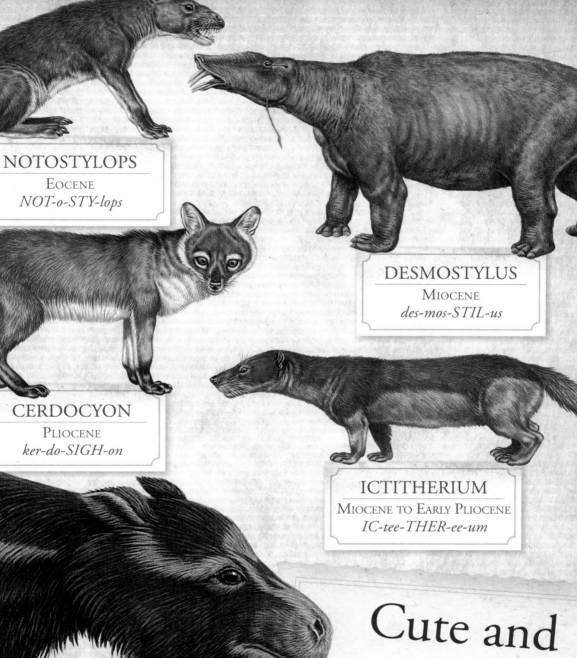

NOTOSTYLOPS
Eocene
NOT-o-STY-lops

DESMOSTYLUS
Miocene
des-mos-STIL-us

CERDOCYON
Pliocene
ker-do-SIGH-on

ICTITHERIUM
Miocene to Early Pliocene
IC-tee-THER-ee-um

MEGATHERIUM
Pleistocene
Meg-a-THER-ee-um

Cute and cuddly

These critters might be soft and furry, but you wouldn't want to get close enough to give one a hug.

SPECTACLED CAIMAN
MODERN

Lots of Crocs

Today's crocodiles look like their ancient relatives, but some of these beasts ate plants!

TELEOSAURUS
MIDDLE JURASSIC
TELL-ee-oh-SAW-rus

TERRESTRISUCHUS
LATE TRIASSIC
ter-EST-ri-SOOK-us

PROTOSUCHUS
EARLY JURASSIC
PROE-toh-SOOK-us

METRIORHYNCHUS

Middle Jurassic to Early Cretaceous
MET-ree-oh-RINK-us

BERNISSARTIA

Early Cretaceous
BER-nih-SART-ee-ah

DEINOSUCHUS

Cretaceous to Pliocene
DINE-oh-SOOK-us

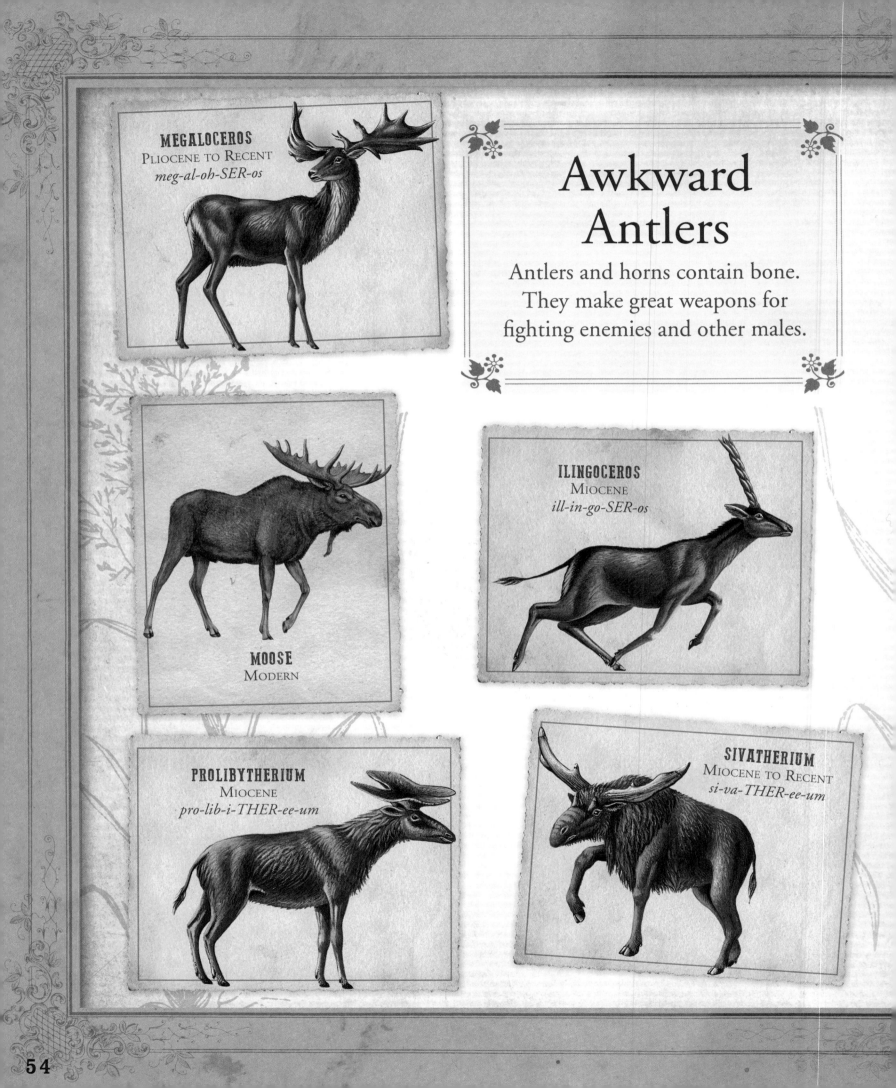

MEGALOCEROS
PLIOCENE TO RECENT
meg-al-oh-SER-os

Awkward Antlers

Antlers and horns contain bone.
They make great weapons for
fighting enemies and other males.

MOOSE
MODERN

ILINGOCEROS
MIOCENE
ill-in-go-SER-os

PROLIBYTHERIUM
MIOCENE
pro-lib-i-THER-ee-um

SIVATHERIUM
MIOCENE TO RECENT
si-va-THER-ee-um

RED DEER
MODERN

SYNDYOCERAS
OLIGOCENE TO MIOCENE
SIN-dee-OSS-er-as

HAYOCEROS
RECENT
hay-oh-SER-os

GREATER KUDU
MODERN

PELOROVIS
PLIOCENE TO RECENT
pel-oh-ROH-vis

EUCLADOCEROS
PLIOCENE TO RECENT
yu-clad-o-SER-os

Extraordinary Necks

Long, strong and bendy necks –
very useful for looking around
corners (and reaching treetops).

GIRAFFE
MODERN

GIRAFFE WEEVIL
MODERN

CERESIOSAURUS
EARLY TRIASSIC
seh-REEZ-ee-oh-SAW-rus

ANSHUNSAURUS
Triassic
an-shun-saw-rus

DROMICEIOMIMUS
Late Cretaceous
dro-MI-see-oh-me-muss

PROTOROSAURUS
Late Permian
PRO-toro-SAW-rus

TANYSTROPHEUS
Triassic
TAN-ee-STROF-ee-us

THEOSODON
Miocene
THEO-so-don

Perfect Pet?

From the past to the present, there have been many fierce cat- and doglike creatures.

SMILODON

Pleistocene to Recent

s-MY-loh-don

DOMESTIC DOG

Modern

CAVE LION

Pleistocene

DINOFELIS

Pliocene to Pleistocene

die-no-FEE-lis

58

EUSMILUS

Eocene to Oligocene
yoo-smy-lus

Can you tell which of these beasts are dogs and which are cats?

MEGANTEREON

Miocene to Pleistocene
meg-an-TER-ee-on

PACHYCROCUTA

Pliocene to Pleistocene
pa-kee-croh-KEW-ta

HESPEROCYON

Eocene to Oligocene
hes-per-oh-SY-on

COLOCOLO

Modern

HEMICYON

Miocene
hem-EE-sy-on

PTERASPIS
Devonian
ter-AP-sis

CLADOSELACHE
Devonian
clad-OH-sel-ACK

PLAICE
Modern

PHARYNGOLEPIS
Silurian
far-IN-gol-EP-is

SCAPANORHYNCHUS
Cretaceous
sca-PAN-or-INK-us

JAMOYTIUS
Silurian
ja-MOY-tee-us

SPATHOBATIS
Jurassic to Cretaceous
SPA-tho-BAT-is

ENCHODUS
Cretaceous to Palaeocene
en-KOH-dus

STETHACANTHUS
Carboniferous
STETH-a-CAN-thus

DREPANASPIS
Devonian
dre-pa-NAS-pis

PLATYSOMUS
Carboniferous to Triassic
PLA-tis-OH-mus

Fabulous Fish

From tiddlers to tyrants, fish have ruled the seas for more than 400 million years.

DIPNORHYNCHUS
Devonian
DIP-nor-RIN-kus

Nice Noses

A collection of snouts, muzzles, proboscises and noses. Pick your favourite!

PTERODAUSTRO
Early Cretaceous
TER-oh-DOW-stro

RYTIODUS
Miocene
RYE-tee-OH-dus

MOERITHERIUM
Eocene to Oligocene
moh-er-ee-THER-ee-um

STENEOFIBER
Eocene to Pliocene
STEN-ee-o-FIB-er

METRIDIOCHOERUS
Pliocene to Recent
me-TRID-ee-oh-ko-AIR-us

KANNEMEYERIA

Early Triassic
KAN-eh-MAY-er-ee-a

CERATOSAURUS

Late Jurassic
ser-at-oh-SAW-rus

MACRAUCHENIA

Miocene to Recent
mac-row-KEEN-ee-a

NORTHERN PIKA

Modern

ANSWERS

MASTERS OF THE AIR

Q: Which of these fluffy fliers was an ancient type of bat?

A: Icaronycteris – it was one of the earliest known bats, but was already very similar to modern bats.

PECULIAR BIRDS

Q: Two of these birds had teeth! Can you spot which ones?

A: Osteodontornis and Archaeopteryx

OSTEODONTORNIS

TERRIBLE TYRANTS

Q: Which of these ferocious reptiles has a venomous bite?

A: The Komodo dragon – scientists haven't found evidence that any dinosaurs were venomous.

FAST MOVERS

Q: Can you spot which of these creatures travelled by gliding?

A: Coelurosauravus – scientists think this small reptile glided between tree branches.

DIMETRODON

BIZARRE BODIES

Q: Which of these creatures used its strange shape to keep warm?

A: Dimetrodon – the large sail on its back would warm up in the sun, and from there, warmed blood would be carried around the rest of its body.

MIGHTY MAMMOTHS

Q: Can you guess which of these giants lived in the coldest places?

A: The woolly mammoth – it had a thick a thick covering of hair to keep warm during the Ice Age.

COBELODUS

INDIAN STRIPED PALM SQUIRREL

SUPER STRIPES

Q: Can you tell which of these beasts were hunters?

A: Cobelodus (ate crustaceans and squid)
Coelophysis (ate small reptiles and the ancestors of mammals)
Ornithomimus (probably ate insects and small animals, as well as fruit and leaves)

PERFECT PET?

Q: Can you tell which of these beasts are dogs and which are cats?

A: Smilodon, Eusmilus, Megantereon, Dinofelis, Colocolo, and the cave lion are all related to cats. The domestic dog and Hesperocyon are both part of the dog family.

HESPEROCYON